J P   ADOFF
             MAKE A
     CIRCLE, KEEP
     US IN

606331

Santa Clara County Free Library

California

Alum Rock	Milpitas { Calaveras / Community Center / Sunnyhills
Campbell	
Cupertino	Morgan Hill
Gilroy	Saratoga { Quito / Village
Los Altos { Main / Woodland	Stanford-Escondido

Research Center-Cupertino

For Bookmobile Service, request schedule

make a circle
keep us
in

poems for a good
day

by arnold adoff / pictures by ronald himler

Library of Congress Cataloging in Publication Data

Adoff, Arnold.
  Make a circle, keep us in.

  SUMMARY: A number of illustrated poems celebrate
the joys of the day: morning, growing up, peanut
butter, hard rain, and thunder.
  [1. American poetry] I. Himler, Ronald, ill.
II. Title.
PZ8.3.A233Mak   811'.5'4   74-22162
ISBN 0-440-05908-9
ISBN 0-440-05909-7 lib. bdg.

for

    Alice
       Jaime
          Virginia
          Leigh

             A.A.

for

    Ann
       Danny
          Anna

             R.H.

morning

           hard
to get
up
   out of the   soft
             warm
             bed

morning
         mean
morning
           who cares
           about your
oat   meal

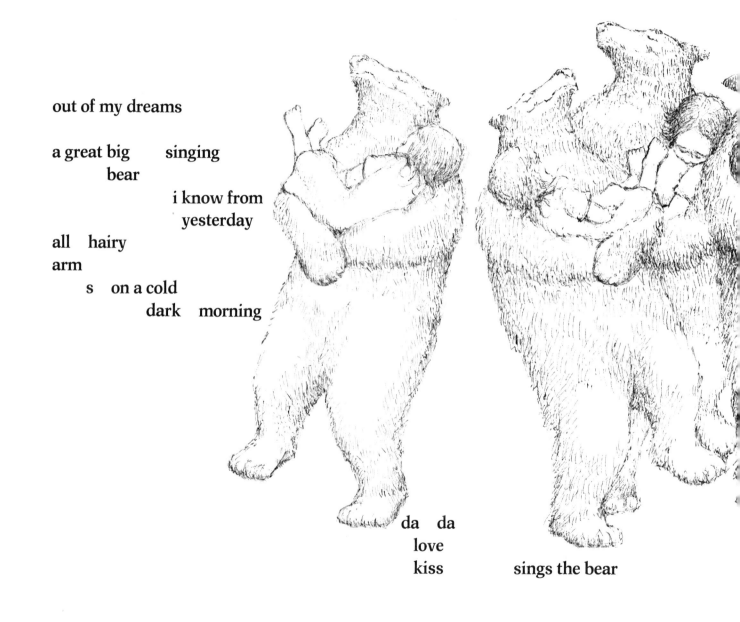

out of my dreams

a great big   singing
               bear

                    i know from
                         yesterday

all   hairy
arm
        s   on a cold
                dark   morning

                                da   da
                                love
                                kiss   sings the bear

da   da
love
honey
cake
face

sings the bear

wet kiss
wake
up
face

honey

nose

ma ma
love
kiss

ma ma
never
miss

toes

da   da
stuffs
them
into   socks   like keys
in   locks

they turn
they turn

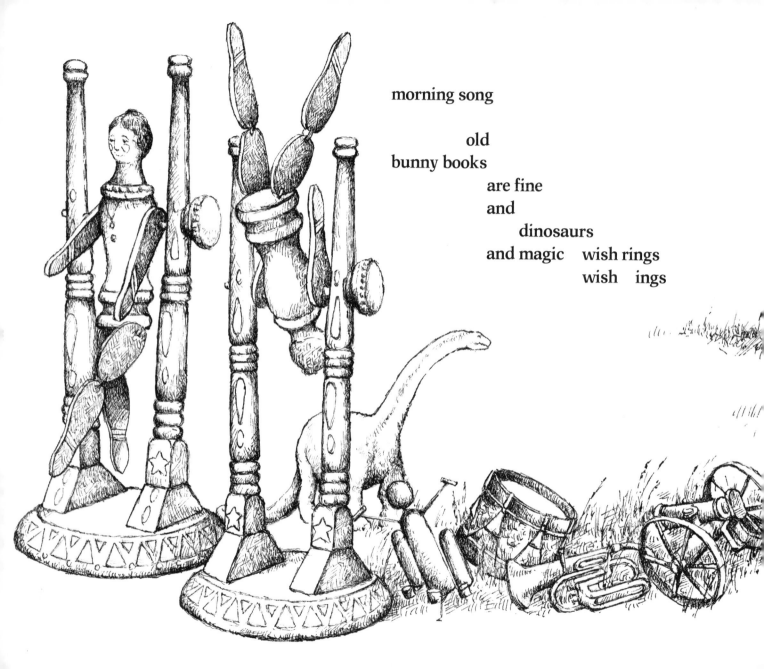

morning song

        old
bunny books
          are fine
and
         dinosaurs
and magic   wish rings
         wish   ings

but i want to grow **up** fast
and be a lawyer
and be a singer

and be a track
                    star
        with
                eight gold
                medals
and never have to put
    my toys away

        just play
        just play

munch

lunch
    at
noon

        peanut
        butter
in
a
s
 poon
        some
        soup
more
milk

ma   ma
    makes

    munch
    lunch

sip

lip   lip
o
slip

lip lip lip
o
slip

lip
o
s l ip

drip
drip
d rip

milk song

da   da
  yells   like bro_{ken}

  bells

       like bro_{ken}

bells
 he
yells

dink
dink   drink
              drink
              drin_k

then his elbow
              knock_s
    his
    coffee in the
              sink

              wink
              wink

just
remember

yells are **loud** but float away
into the air up to the
roof or out the windows

hugs are **solid** arms that rest
around your shoulders and
hold you in the quiet time

grandpa in march

goes   around
            the house
               each
               day

and feels the
       ground
and pinches
            twigs
and   digs
and   digs

pushing
spring

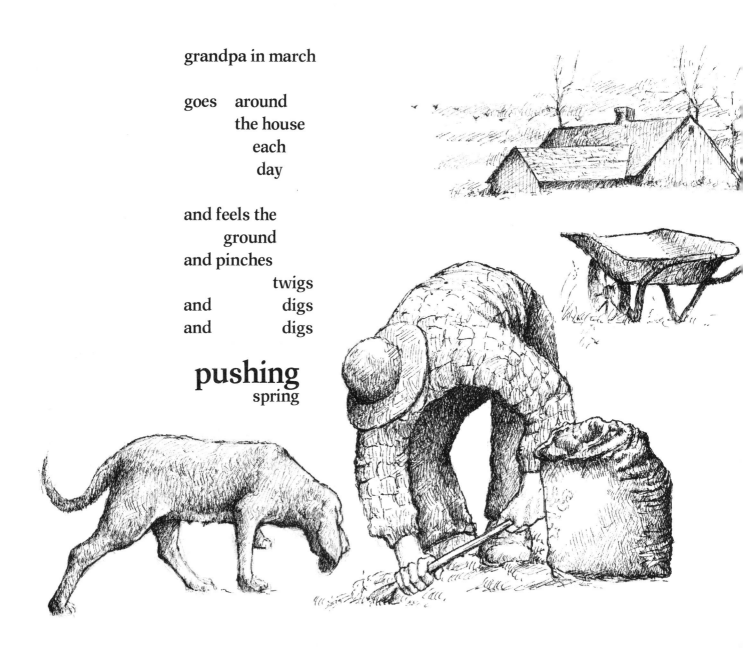

run

trip
rip ip
     r
        ip

new
pants

smac**k**

snea**k**

attac**k**

ma ma
means
that

n o
sm o k e
o
o
o
da o da
you
bad

dad

this early afternoon

the chicken
is in the pan
and the yams
are boiling in the pot

a lot of work for sunday
dinner
and a little time before
the biscuits and the greens

beans
are a snap for me
at the kitchen table
as grandma sits
and   knits
and
knits

and tells a sunday dinner story
about marching women long ago   with flags
and brave old songs

and grandma knits
and   knits

she fits

tub time

and time

enough
to **scrub**
and **rub**
and **rub**

all bub
bles
bub

bub
blub
as i stand tall

look
i
am g r o w i n g uP

and when will you

gro
w

dow
n

da da
  love
   kis
     h

m s   u h
  u hm s
m   s   h
  u   h m u s
m u s h
mushmushmus
          h

mush mush
    brushbrush
         b r
           ush

      mush
      tash

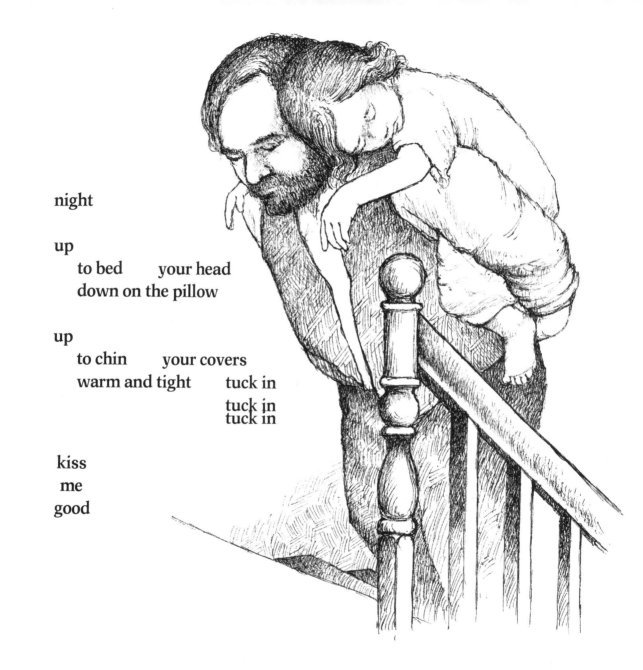

night

up
    to bed   your head
    down on the pillow

up
    to chin   your covers
    warm and tight   tuck in
                    tuck in
                    tuck in

kiss
 me
good

quiet   quiet
quiet

da   da
on
a
diet

no   cookies   cakes
or   bread
he   chews his carrot
sticks instead

and puffs his stalks of celery
like green cigars
and cries
and
cri es

but late at night
he eats a piece
of pie

i see

in
the
mid   dle
of
the
mid   dle
of
the
mid   dle
of
the   night

light   n n
          i g
        and a
          full
          bed

ma   ma
    hug
tight   n n
        i g

thunder

hands like
       bands
     of steel

    around
  are round

make a circle
keep   us
      in

hard rain

  ma   ma
   says
               it is good
for the
  trees

and hugs
and **hugs**

i sit
you sit
sit
ting   we

waiting for the storm
to
be

some
place
else

a chocolate
m $_u$ s $_h$ t $_a$ s $_h$

for
the
brave

and cookies
under covers

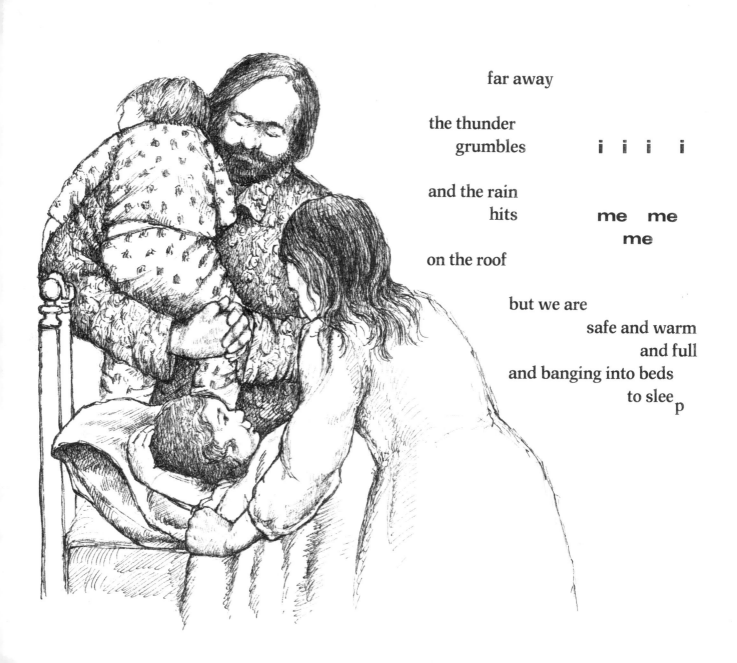

far away

the thunder
grumbles   i i i i

and the rain
hits   **me** **me**
me

on the roof

but we are
safe and warm
and full
and banging into beds
to slee$_p$

we are
        each with each
and stronger than a show
                off
                storm

        we are

        we

About the Author

Arnold Adoff is an anthologist and poet who is well-known for the uniqueness of his work and who seeks to find a new visual and verbal means of expression. Here, as in his two previous picture books *(MA nDA LA* and *Black   is brown   is tan),* each word is like a musical note that leads the eye and the mind through the poems. Mr. Adoff lives in Yellow Springs, Ohio, with his wife, novelist Virginia Hamilton, and their two children. Among his anthologies are *Brothers and Sisters* and *Black Out Loud,* which are available in Dell Laurel-Leaf paperback editions.

About the Artist

Ronald Himler has illustrated many books for children, among them *Morris Brookside, a Dog,* available in a Yearling edition. With each new book, Mr. Himler tries to use a technique which will best define the text. Here, his pen and ink create a bold line, representing the solidity of a family; his delicate cross-hatching softens and molds the characters. Mr. Himler lives in New York City with his wife, Ann, and their children.

About the Book

This book has been designed by Lynn Braswell to enhance the words in the poems and to heighten their visual form. The text has been set on film in Vladimir, Vladimir bold, Versatile 73 and Versatile 75 in sizes ranging from 9 pt. through 28 pt.